Th
Fishing

a brief history

Dave Smart

Tor Mark Press · Penryn

Other books in the Tor Mark series

China clay - traditional mining methods in Cornwall
Cornish mining industry - a brief history
Cornish folklore
Cornish legends
Cornish mining - underground
Cornish mining - at surface
Cornish recipes
Cornish saints
Cornwall's early lifeboats
Cornwall's engine houses
Cornwall's railways
Cornwall's structure and scenery
Customs and superstitions from Cornish folklore
Demons, ghosts and spectres in Cornish folklore
Exploring Cornwall with your car
Harry Carter - Cornish smuggler
Houses, castles and gardens in Cornwall
Introducing Cornwall
Old Cornwall - in pictures
Shipwrecks around Land's End
Shipwrecks around the Lizard
Shipwrecks around Mounts Bay
Shipwrecks - St Ives to Bude
South-east Cornwall
The story of Cornwall
The story of Cornwall's churches
The story of the Cornish language
The story of St Ives
The story of Truro Cathedral
Surfing South-west
Tales of the Cornish fishermen
Tales of the Cornish miners
Tales of the Cornish smugglers
Tales of the Cornish wreckers
Twelve walks on the Lizard
Victorian Cornwall

This edition first published 1992 by Tor Mark Press,
Islington Wharf, Penryn, Cornwall TR10 8AT

© 1992 Tor Mark Press

ISBN 0-85025-331-4

Acknowledgements

The author and publishers are grateful to the following for permission to reproduce photographs:

Channel Foods page 32; Royal Institution of Cornwall pages 5 (both), 8, 13, 15, 16-17, 18, 19 (both), 21, 22, 23, 24-25, 26; Spectrum Studio, Newlyn, page 31; Billy Stephenson pages 6, 20, 28 & 29; Paul White page 30 (both).

Other photographs are from the author's or publishers' own collections.

The author is grateful to Mr Les Douch, for his patience in checking and correcting the captions to the illustrations, and to his wife Pauline for reading through the various drafts of the text

Printed in Great Britain by Swannack Brown & Co Ltd, Hull

2

1 The industry in 1600

Exactly when fishing in Cornwall became an industry is impossible to say, but by the time Richard Carew published his *Survey of Cornwall* in 1602 it was of national importance. Detailed records of shipments earlier than the sixteenth century are rare. Records of exploratory shipments of pilchards in very small quantities do exist but by 1555 shipments of pilchards from Looe are clearly recorded and the export of these and other fish, chiefly hake, was established. Many tons of 'pickled' and other 'dry' pilchards were shipped to La Rochelle, Bordeaux, St Tropos, Leghorn (Livorno), Genoa and other Mediterranean ports.

Hake and pilchards were also shipped to Nantes as early as 1570.

Carew in his *Survey* describes the types of fish that may be caught and the various methods of catching them. Peal, trout, grilse and salmon, all able to live in both salt and fresh water, were mostly taken with a hoop net, fastened on the river bed with its wide mouth open, facing upstream. This net trapped fish in much the same way as the wicker 'kypes' used until recently on the river Severn.

Salmon could also be caught with the hook and line, 'where they use either flies for their bait, or the salmon's spear, a weapon like Neptune's mace or trident'. Another profitable means of taking trout was by 'hutches', whereby a head of stones was first placed across the river: a grating of laths, sharpened at the end, trapped and impaled the salmon.

Other 'round' fish were caught in weirs of wicker or wattle, in 'haking nets' stretched across the mud of an estuary between stakes, and in 'tuck' and 'trammel' nets. But it was the sein or seine net which yielded the greatest number of fish such as mackerel, pilchard and herring.

The seine is a net about forty fathom in length with which they encompass a part of the sea, and draw the same on land by two ropes fastened at his ends, together with such fish as lighteth within his precinct.

Carew then compares the 'drovers' or drivers with the seiners whose larger nets were cast out in the open sea, as opposed to the small seines within a harbour or cove. These longer seine nets were laid out by three or four boats each manned by six men, directed by a 'huer' who

. . . standeth on the cliff side and from thence best discerneth the quantity and course of the pilchards, according whereunto he cundeth [directs] the master of each boat, by crying with a loud voice, whistling through his fingers, and wheazing certain diversified and significant signs with a bush which he holdeth in his hand . . . . At his appointment they cast out their net, draw it to either hand as the shoal lieth or fareth [moves], beat with their oars to keep in the fish, and at last either close or tuck it up in the sea, or draw the same on land with more certain profit, if the ground be not rough of rocks.

Drift nets were used by other fishermen known as 'drovers' or drivers, and there was controversy between the two:

The seiners complain with open mouth that these drovers work much prejudice to the commonwealth of fishermen, and reap thereby small gain to themselves; for the taking of some few breaketh and scattereth the whole shoal and [discourages] them from approaching the shore; neither are those taken merchantable, by reason of their bruising in the mesh. Let the crafts-masters decide the controversy.

In fact the controversy continued until both seines and drivers were obsolete; many arguments and brawls occurred. Magistrates were fairly lenient about such disputes.

Whether the pilchards were caught by seines or drift nets, they were brought on shore. Some were sold fresh, but most were bought by merchants for preservation and taken to pilchard cellars. These were built of local granite, and still survive in many Cornish harbours. The pilchards were

. . . first salted and piled up row by row in square heaps on the ground in some cellar, which they term bulking, where they remain for some ten days until the superfluous moisture of the blood and salt be soaked from them.

The salt was saved for further use, and the fish were then either fumed, pressed or pickled. According to Carew, 'an infinite number of women and children' went to work overnight after a catch, and 'a lusty housewife may earn three shillings in a night', which was in those days a week's pay for a labourer.

Pilchards destined for France were pickled – packed in hogsheads without further treatment. For the hotter climates of Spain and Italy smoking to make fumadoes (hence the local name fermades or 'fair maids') had been common but was no longer so, probably because there were too many fish for this slower treatment. Most of the pilchards were placed in hogsheads pierced with holes and pressed with heavy weights until the oil ran out of them. This 'train oil' was carefully preserved.

In 1600 some 95% of the casks were exported, and the price of pilchards had risen because of the export demand. Casks were becoming expensive and a statute had been made in 1584 to oblige merchants to import to

There are alas no illustrations of the industry in 1600, but these scenes from the late nineteenth and early twentieth centuries may not be far different.

Above: With the seine net full, baskets of pilchards are dipped out of the sea into small boats
called dippers, St Ives, c. 1900
Below: Salt is added to the pilchards before they are put into the tanks, Sennen 1907

Overleaf: Packing pilchards into hogsheads, Fox's Cellar, Newlyn, 1925. The vertical
pressing poles were gradually screwed down to press out the 'train' oil

Cornwall the same amount of wood as they were exporting in cask form.

Carew says that when a catch was made, local people arrived with horses and panniers to carry the fresh fish inland. Some 'jowsters' used baskets slung over their backs, supported by a strap across their foreheads, in which they hawked the fish to inland villages and farms. Small quantities of pilchards were (and indeed sometimes still are) packed in a 'bussa' or earthenware jar, and pickled in brine for use in winter. The train oil was burned in a 'chill', a coarse pottery lamp which provided light for the cottage. (One can be seen in the museum of the Royal Institution of Cornwall in Truro.)

Other fish, especially predators following the pilchards such as hake, tunny and blue sharks, were caught accidentally in the seine nets; Carew describes other methods of fishing, with line and bait, with baskets for wrasse, and on the north coast (where there are few safe harbours) an ingenious automatic boat to lay out the net:

> They have a device of two sticks filled with corks and crossed flatlong, out of whose midst there riseth a third, and at the same hangeth a sail; to this engine, termed a lestercock, they tie one end of their bolter (a long line with hooks attached) so as the wind coming from the shore filleth the sail and carrieth the bolter out into the sea, which, after the respite of some hours, is drawn in again by a cord fastened at the nearer end.

2 How this industry developed

In 1582 there were nearly 2000 seafaring men in Cornwall, more than any other county except Devon, and the trade was improving fast. The Market House in Penzance was built in 1615, and by 1673 the market was busy with 'fish in great plenty' and merchants coming from Penryn and Falmouth to buy. Boats came from London to collect cured pilchards. But the busiest harbours in the seventeenth century were St Ives, Padstow and Looe. Only six boats were registered at Penzance itself in 1665.

Few records have survived from the seventeenth century giving details of the landings at the various ports but records of salt cellars at Fowey exist, as do records of agreements dated 1668-70 in which men agreed to serve as seiners for the forthcoming pilchard season. They were paid 3s.8d. a month with a further £1.14s.6d. to be paid at the end of the year! This was in contrast to the later method, of share payments based on the value of the catch.

Between 1600 and 1640 there were considerable and very frightening acts of piracy on the open seas involving fishing boats. Pirates from North Africa, locally referrred to as 'Turks', were coming close to shore and taking many fishermen back to Algeria and Morocco to serve as slaves. Insurance against such losses became expensive for boat owners, and local families were reluctant to send their men to sea. Some men were taken from within their own harbours at night, Looe suffering particularly badly in 1626 when a hundred men were taken! Ransoms of between £50 and £500 were demanded by the 'Turks' for the return of each man.

Hundreds of fishermen also went to Newfoundland, often for twelve months or more, fishing for cod which had been found in enormous quantities. This practice ceased at the beginning of the nineteenth century.

Back in home waters, pilchard and mackerel continued to be the main catches. The season for pilchard fishing was from late July through the winter – traditionally between harvest and hallowe'en – depending on the appearance of the shoals. Mackerel fishing began in March and normally lasted four to six months, but they were also caught between September and December.

When larger fish were caught, they were often processed to be sent outside Cornwall. Dried, smoked or salted fish were a delicacy to people living well inland. Ling and cod were fairly easy to dry, especially in summer, but skates and rays required special treatment, owing to their urea content and the subsequent formation of ammonia. Many were cut and hung outside cottages to dry in the sun. Dried fish were easy to pack and were dispatched to distant markets by cart or boat.

Skate hanging out to dry, Bunker's Hill, St Ives, 1900. Their livers were sometimes saved as a delicacy

Many types of small boat were built in Cornwall. The seine boats were low, broad in the beam and sharp in the bows. The boats which laid drift nets were mainly 'luggers' with masts fore and aft. Mounts Bay and St Ives boats varied slightly in mast position and East Cornwall luggers differed again, having squared transoms rather than pointed sterns.

Gigs, shorter and narrower than seine boats, had a crew of four including the cox and were fast. They were used for handlining for mackerel, ling and hake, and occasionally seining for mullet. Nowadays these attractive gigs are used only for pleasure in Cornwall and the Isles of Scilly.

Other industries flourished as the numbers of fishermen increased – boatbuilders and coopers, rope and net makers. Melinda Sampson and her mother from Mousehole used to make cod 'ends' with rope suspended from a rail in her living room as recently as the late 1970s, but this practice seems now to have ceased.

Virtually the entire community in a fishing port was involved directly in the industry and, with many back yards and cellars converted to bulking houses, walls and floors encrusted with salt, fish scales and the general detritus of a flourishing industry, the fishy smells can only be imagined!

Most ports were continuing to flourish in the mid-eighteenth century. A contract book of 1759 gives us a glimpse of some of the details:

25th April 1759

Contracted with Frances Robert, Orchard Cranken, Prudence Yeoman, Dorcas Wiley and Mary Matthew to cure fish at Mousehole at 2d. per hogshead and to pay half of the carriage of all seine fish which they shall not be able to carry themselves and to look after the drift boats as usual.

A hogshead was a large cask which contained about 3000 pilchards and weighed about four hundredweight. Another agreement was made on 28 April with the cellar women of Newlyn:

We whose names are hereunto subscribed do acknowledge to have this day agreed with Mr Wm. Veale and the Rev'd Mr Thos. Carlyon to salt, case, break out and put into hogsheads fit for exportation all the tithe pilchards and herrings within the town of Newlyn at 2d. per hogshead and also to be at the charge of one half of the carriage of all pilchards and herrings taken by the seiner which they shall not be able to carry themselves, and likewise to attend the driving boats and carry all drift fish as former women did in the late Mr Wm. Gwavas's time.

The sign of: Mary Cock, Mary Richards, Elizabeth Legh, Mary Tonkin, Dorothy Tonkin, Phillis Maddren, Eleanor Tonkin and Jane Paul

Witness: Thos. Paul

Edward and Joseph Downing were also employed to move pilchards at a set price:

. . . to ship all the tithe pilchards made in Newlyn at 6d. per hogshead anywhere in Mount's Bay and also all the trash [damaged pilchards] at the same price per cask to take them from the cellar doors after being viewed by the Salt Officer.

'Tithe fish' were the percentage claimed by the Church. It is clear that there was considerable organisation in dealing first with the fresh pilchards as they came ashore and then the pressed pilchards. Yet most of these working people could not write their own names, and each signed with a different monogram.

The 'waste' salt was used again if it was of satisfactory condition. An indication of the increased volume of pilchard processing is the import of French salt – in 1764 800 bushels to Mousehole and 1800 bushels to Newlyn.

The accounts show a shipment of train oil, shipped to London by Messrs Veale and Carlyon on board the *Charming Nancy*, Chris Hocking master, of '8 casks totalling 456 gallons made (net) £34.1s.6d.'

In the Newlyn seine accounts for the week 17-22 July 1765 we find:

Success seine	151 baskets
Happy Return seine	135 baskets
Speedwell seine	33 baskets
St Peter seine	461 baskets
Vernon seine	107 baskets
Fortune seine	319 baskets
Content seine	63 baskets
Endeavour seine	103 baskets
Cumberland seine	131 baskets

This made a total of 137 hogsheads. At Mousehole at the same time five seines produced 70 hogsheads. These were all sold to Mr Batten, some at 10/- and some at 6s.6d. per hogshead and shipped from Newlyn.

In February 1764 an agent, Mr Thomas Tremearne, was asked to find the 'best market' for pilchards at Alicante, Valencia or Genoa, or whichever port he thought gave the best price. The good ship *Acorn* exported 386 hogsheads of pilchards from St Ives on 6 October 1795, bound for Venice. The master, Thornton Fisher, made it clear on the Bill of Lading that they were 'condition unknown' to him: in the unlikely event of the cargo deteriorating or being unacceptable to the purchasers, the master could not then be held responsible.

Records also exist of the ownership of cellars and seines at the end of the eighteenth century and the beginning of the nineteenth. Normally each fisherman received a share of the value of the catch, and the boat also received a share to pay for repairs and new equipment.

Among the seine fishermen, who were certainly wealthier than the drifter men, some received a guaranteed weekly wage, and the partners divided the profit from the catch. The boats were a capital investment by the partners and repairs and replacements demanded further capital. The typical partnership owned three boats, two nets and premises on shore for preparing the catch. Their nets were huge, at least a quarter of a mile long and 33 yards deep. The partnership generally employed a huer on the cliffs, who might have a hut (one of which is still to be seen just outside Newquay) and whose cry of 'Hevva!' when he sighted a shoal brought the whole town to life.

Evidence of these partnerships can be seen in the accounts of the Blewitt's seine and the Smith's cellars in Marazion. On 25 December 1800, the Blewitt's seine was leased to William Gluyas and Sons. He was granted a $\frac{5}{64}$ share, and similar parts were granted to John Edwards of Hayle, Richard Oxnam of Penzance, Thomas Grylls of Helston, Sampson Thomas of Marazion and George James Matthews of St Michael's Mount.

Bulking pilchards at 'Maid Betsy's cellar, St Ives, 1871. Was the gentleman in the top hat, left of centre, in charge here? A 'gurry' or wheel-less barrow is in use lower left

$\frac{1}{8}$ of the Smith's cellars in Marazion, also in the possession of William Gluyas the younger and Oliver Gluyas at Marazion were also leased along with $\frac{20}{60}$ of the Blewitt cellars on St Michael's Mount.

Without on-shore facilities, no fishing industry could develop. Suggestions were made in 1819 by James Brown of Mylor, an ex-pilot and superintendent of the Scottish herring fishery, to provide facilities on the Isles of Scilly for processing catches and treating nets and lines. He also recommended training some of the islanders as pilots, and using their gigs to guide ships in the area away from dangerous rocks; these men could fish for cod and ling when not otherwise employed. The gigs were used but due to the isolated nature of the islands no real industry developed, and to this day most of the catches are brought to the mainland for auction.

The problems of early nineteenth century fishing ports included cholera and other diseases, the condition of roads and trackways, and the fluctuation of the prices for fish. Here are some entries from the diary of John Short of St Ives:

Wed 2nd June 1852
Boats landed from 500 - 800 fish (pilchards); sold at 5s.6d. and 6/- per 100/120.
A great number of herring which sold at $\frac{1}{2}$ d. each, at the rate of 5/- per 100.

Wed 6th October 1852
Boats caught from 300 - 3000 mackerel; sold at 10/- and 9/- per 100.
Carrack Gladden caught fish.
Tremearne & Co missed.
Messrs Wearnes & Co missed.
Messrs Bolitho & Co missed.
Messrs Bolitho & Co caught about 20 gurries [see photo, page 11].
Boats reported gone ashore. A schooner ran aground laden with salt from Liverpool.

Friday 17th December 1852
Boats on the drift took from 3000 - 6000 fine pilchards which sold at 1s.9d. per 100.
Some few hundred herrings which sold at 3/- per 100.

Thursday 5th May 1853
400 - 2000 pilchards sold at 10/- to 16/- per 100, to the Bristol and Plymouth buyers.

Thursday 11 September 1856
1000 - 11,000 pilchards sold
600 small mackerel sold (in pilchard nets).
Sold at 8s.6d. per 100 mackerel.
Sold at 1s.6d. per 100 pilchards.

Even this isolated report indicates that the price could fluctuate according to the quantities landed. This was a source of constant misunderstanding and misinterpretation by the fishermen who genuinely believed that the merchants would make more money out of them if they were paid less when there were heavy landings. It was actually the operation of the law of supply and demand, but it remains a problem to this day.

Weighing fish at Polperro, c. 1870. The boxes have Billingsgate markings

3 The industry in the late nineteenth century

Much remained unchanged in 1890, when tourists and artists began to 'discover' Cornwall. Thousands of hogsheads of pilchards were still being sent to Italy through the ports of Naples and Genoa, and indeed the Newlyn firm British Cured Pilchards was still in 1990 sending pilchards to Italy, though by road. The hub of the pilchard industry had moved in the mid-nineteenth century from the south coast between Plymouth and Mevagissey to the west Cornwall coast.

One great change had occurred, however, which was a catalyst of further change; in 1859 the railways of Cornwall were connected to the national railway system. This was a golden opportunity for Cornish industries to develop. Although the marketing techniques of the fishing industry needed improvement, important new markets were opened up.

Auction outside what is now Newlyn Post Office, early 1900s. The fish appear to be laid out for individual sale

At the same time, complex change was occurring in catching methods. Drifters and seiners were working side by side and, when the railway opened, both increased in numbers to satisfy 'up-country' demand, and all species of pelagic fish (those which swim near the surface, including pilchard, herring and mackerel) were caught in greater numbers. The boats went further afield, often beyond the Isles of Scilly. But on a day calm enough for fishing, they might not be able to return in time for the fish train at Penzance, in which case the fish had lost some of their shine by the time they reached market.

The first solution was the use of a single fast steamer, which took all the catches back to Penzance to catch the afternoon train, enabling the boats to continue fishing. Over the next few years transporting fish on the railways became big business with rival companies setting up their own systems for landing and transporting the catch. Once landed, the fish were washed and packed as speedily as possible, especially in the summer months, into wicker baskets with straw as packing. Specialist merchants dealt with the intricacies of marketing a large variety of species; their availablity at this time was constantly changing as catching methods and techniques began to change rapidly.

Men, women and children turn out to see the catches arrive on the beach, St Ives, c. 1900

Hundreds of horse-drawn carts came daily from fishing towns and villages to the rail terminus at Penzance, bringing ready boxed fish. In the first six months of 1861, only two years after the rail connection, over 1000 tons of fish was carried by rail in Cornwall. As the traffic grew, specially designed fish wagons were built. There was full employment in the industry as long as the weather allowed the boats to go out.

Ice became necessary when fish was transported by rail for long distances, and also on the boats when they began to stay at sea for longer periods. At first enormous chunks of Arctic ice were brought down by sea, broken up and stored in huge chilly warehouses in the larger ports such as Newlyn; around 1900 a method was discovered for freezing fresh water, and ice was then crushed and mixed with the catch on the boats. As catching methods improved, and new markets were opened up, competition among the merchants became keener. At Billingsgate, with fish arriving from all over England, it was fish which arrived in peak condition and at the right time which received the top prices.

One unfortunate aspect of the opening of the railway was the isolation of fishing communities not within reach of the terminus at Penzance. Boats continued to fish from small coves on both north and south coast, but it

Carts and jowsters crowd the Newlyn beach waiting for the day's landings

The donkey cart in the foreground is from the nearby village of Paul

Here a horse and cart is being loaded with fish directly out of the boat, St Ives, c. 1900

was uneconomic to take the fish to a railway station. Even where there was a station accessible, it did not have the specialist loading facilities which were by now necessary. Until road transport improved, these fishing villages declined; the fish could only be sold to the local community. Many Cornish people survived on a diet of salted or dried fish; lines were put out when pilchard and mackerel were not being caught, and good quality cod, hake, ling and skate were brought ashore.

Industrial fishing began to be dominated by a few fishing ports. The fishing villages which had become ports all had good sheltered natural harbours, and potential for pier construction. Newquay, Padstow, St Michael's Mount, Newlyn, Mousehole and Bude all had pier or quay construction as early as the 14th or 15th centuries. In the 19th century increased quay construction took place at Porthleven, Polperro, Mousehole, Mevagissey, St Ives and Newlyn.

It was Newlyn which was to develop as the main port in the south-west. Its advantages were proximity to rich fishing grounds and to the rail terminus, and a large local population which had been committed to fishing for centuries. The new South Pier was opened in 1886 so that boats could now moor up here instead of in the bay or on ropes in the central harbour area. An even longer North Pier was completed in 1894, enabling every boat to tie up alongside the quay for safety. At last it seemed that life for the local fishermen would be easier, but a new problem lay ahead. The port facilities were now so good that they began to attract other fishermen from outside Cornwall!

These nets on Polperro breakwater (above) have been 'barked', probably in the hut beside them. New nets were treated with oak bark to tan and preserve them, as below at St Ives, c. 1880

Pilchard drivers (luggers) leaving Newlyn for the fishing grounds, c. 1900

4 Competition

Fleets of east coast boats began to arrive on the Cornish fishing grounds between 1860 and 1870. By 1878 there were about 100 east coast trawlers fishing in south-west waters, as well as steam drifters. A steam-powered fishing boat had been built at Hayle in 1876, and proved her worth many times when the sailing vessels were becalmed, but it was more than thirty years before Newlyn had its first steam drifter, the *Speedwell*, by which time there were 200 steam drifters on the east coast. The Cornish fisherman's reluctance to change from sail to steam was not purely conservatism. The east coast ports were near enough to coal fields to have the benefit of cheap coal, whereas in Cornwall coal had to be brought from South Wales and was expensive. The boiler and fuel supply in a steamer also took up a great deal of space which could have been devoted to the catch.

For some 250 years, Cornish fishermen had observed the religious command not to work on Sundays; the spread of Methodism had strengthened this attitude, and everyone observed the strict preachings of the local minister. Only rarely did someone who had had a bad week's fishing give

When bad weather approached, as here, the luggers filled St Ives harbour, so that you could almost walk across it stepping from boat to boat

way to temptation if a large shoal of pilchards was sighted on a Sunday.

The east coast men did not accept this local custom, and brought fish ashore on Monday mornings, so it made a good price because there was no competition from the Cornishmen. This was a cause of dispute for many years, and culminated in riots in Newlyn and Penzance in 1896. The riots started on 18 May and continued for several days. When the east coast men tried to land their catches, there were pitched battles with the Newlyn men. The local police could not quell the riot and 300 men of the Royal Berkshire Regiment were urgently called in from Plymouth.

Although people were injured and various Newlyn men appeared in court, no heavy sentences were imposed; but the troops and police maintained their presence to keep law and order because there were still about a hundred east coast boats at sea. Eventually calm was restored and in time the problem was forgotten.

The east coast men had always argued that to abstain from fishing on one day of the week meant a loss of earnings to the crew; their boats were expensive, and needed to be worked intensively to be profitable. By 1903 even the Newlyn boats were working on Sundays. They had reconsidered

Wet fish being packed in baskets and boxes on the quayside in front of the Sloop Inn, St Ives, in 1904

the issue, possibly prompted by the refusal of the Home Secretary to support the Newlyn case: although there was a local custom to refrain from fishing, it was not actually illegal. St Ives, however, continued Sunday observance and disputes continued until 1929. Although many of the east coast men preferred to land their catches at St Ives, because of the direct rail link, they eventually transferred to Newlyn making it the undisputed premier fishing port in the south-west. Local allied industries were grateful for the extra income from the ever increasing number of visiting boats.

When internal combustion engines first became available, between 1905 and 1920, the Cornishmen were quick to see their advantages. The earliest engines ran on paraffin, although they were pre-heated on a petrol/paraffin mixture. Much less space was taken up by engine and fuel than with steam power, and they were much cleaner and easier to maintain. Later, diesel engines were used, though not until after 1945. The size of engine increased from 7 Hp to 26 Hp, and eventually to the 250 Hp diesels used today.

With power, boats could now go to sea in weather which would be dangerous to sailing boats and could motor home without the frustration of being becalmed or suffering an adverse wind.

More and more fish had to be caught in the shortest possible time to meet the demands of the market. More trawlers began to arrive from the east coast to fish on the well-stocked banks to the far west of the Isles of Scilly. All these improvements resulting in larger catches did not always mean that fishermen's incomes rose. When catches were greatest, prices fell because consumers could only eat a certain amount of fish in a given time. And with no management of the fisheries as we know it today, it seems that no one reflected on the stocks of individual species. Were the seas around our coasts an inexhaustible resource?

Emptying crab pots and preparing floats in Mullion, 1908

5 The decline of the pilchard industry

As the drift net fishery increased, and steam-powered trawlers made it possible to catch larger fish such as cod, ling, hake, conger and pollack, the pilchard seine-fishing industry was doomed. Demand for pilchards dropped, and it was no longer economic to maintain seine or drift net fleets. The pilchard shoals were also less numerous, possibly because of changes in salinity, mineral content and sea currents.

Cornish fishermen, however, blamed the trawlers for breaking up pelagic shoals and destroying young stock. This is something which even modern scientific research would find difficult to prove either way. Another reason for the demise of the pilchard trade has been the vast imports from West Africa, where they are caught and canned in enormous quantities very cheaply.

St Ives folk are unlikely to see such a scene as this again, though the fathers of elderly people in the town may well have been involved in 'tucking' pilchards in the heyday of the industry

Although pilchards were still being caught with drift nets as recently as the 1930s, boats were going further and further afield to locate them. Once landed they could be sold locally, salted for the Italian market, or put into cans. Until quite recently there was a canning factory in Newlyn for pilchards and mackerel, which would be mixed with tomato sauce or brine. They could also be minced and made into fish paste. Many even went for fish-meal to ports such as Avonmouth or Bristol.

By the early decades of the twentieth century, many buildings used for pilchard processing had been converted to stores, the seine boats tied up and the nets piled in lofts, many rotting there to this day. It was the end of a grand era in the history of the fishing community in Cornwall.

Families who wished to continue fishing but could not afford a steam drifter had various options. One was to invest in a set of 'withy' baskets of long-lines. A tall basket was filled with a continuous line which had anything up to 150 'strops' attached to it at regular intervals. At the end of each strop, which was about two feet in length, was tied a large swivel hook

It was recorded that 653 hogsheads of pilchards were loaded in Penzance onto this vessel, the SS *Adria*, bound for the Mediterranean

which could be baited with mackerel or pilchard. The long-line was thrown over the side to lie on the sea-bed overnight. The beginning and end of the line would be marked at the surface with 'danns' – large floats of cork topped with a coloured flag. This method of fishing brought many fine specimens of hake, cod, ling and conger. The only disadvantage was that other species could feed off the hooked fish: many a specimen would be raised to the surface with chunks of flesh missing as a result of predators. This method continued in use until the 1970s. Large specimens fetched a good price up country, and finding good ground, particularly over wrecks, brought out the true hunting spirit in local men!

6 The twentieth century

Since the early 1900s, the patterns of catching, handling and marketing fish in Cornwall have changed dramatically, in ways partly described in previous chapters. Traditional methods of catching with seines, drift nets and long-lines using sailing boats were superceded by trawls and motor powered vessels. Ice superceded brine, smoking and drying. The demands of merchants in the large cities led to a more sophisticated approach to the packing and marketing of freshly caught fish, and this aspect of the industry is continually being improved with the introduction of new materials for packing, freezing and storing. Transport facilities are also improving steadily.

The pilchard is not the only species to have declined in importance. The herring fishery suffered from an influx of French trawlers around the turn of the century, and their activities, together with those of Plymouth based trawlers, are said to have decimated the herring stocks particularly on the north coast. Herring could still be caught in the North Sea, where several hundred drifters were active, until stocks dwindled there too and in the mid 1970s a total ban on herring fishing was enforced. As a result of this ban the stocks eventually recovered and there are now thriving herring fisheries in the North Sea and off the coast of Norway. There is still a demand for 'kippered' herrings but much of the catch is now processed to make rollmops, Bismarck, spiced herring and other such delicacies.

The third pelagic species caught in quantity was the mackerel, and upwards of 400 Cornish mackerel drivers and 200 steam drifters at work in the late nineteenth century clearly affected stocks. The fishery virtually closed in the 1930s, and by the 1960s stocks had naturally improved again. Hundreds of small boats and several of the new 'purse-seiners' arrived off the Cornish coast. These modern seiners have nets wound on a huge drum and paid out through a gantry on the stern of the vessel. The smaller boats used lengths of line with fifteen feathers concealing hooks attached, held by hand over the side and moved up and down in the water. This may sound primitive, but thousands of tons of mackerel were landed this way each year until the early 1980s. They were either sold fresh, smoked or frozen, catering for a new wave of demand for this relatively cheap and prolific fish.

Smaller fish were also caught in purse seines, mainly finding their way to factories to be processed as fish fertilizer or animal feed, and this continues today whenever large enough shoals are brought ashore.

Full to the gunwhales: the crew of the *Efficient*, Newlyn, at the peak of the 1976 mid-water trawling season

Throughout the twentieth century there have been further increases in the number of boats in the fleets, as local fishermen have felt obliged to match the catching ability of their east coast rivals. Groups of fishermen and merchants, both local and from other parts of the country, were keen to invest in faster trawlers, improved nets and technologically advanced equipment.

Even the shellfish industry has benefited from the introduction of motor crabbers with motorised winches to haul up the pots. After a short burst of lobster and crawfish fishing by local divers in the 1960s, the industry picked up, though greater and greater numbers of pots for both crabs and lobsters are needed to keep the industry viable. The latest system of net fishing for crawfish has increased the catching capacity, though the actual number landed still seems to be dwindling.

Throughout the twentieth century, fishing communities have been slow to adapt to new fishing methods, and demand for different species. Nowadays the distant water fishing grounds towards the edge of the continental shelf are being scoured for stocks of high-value fish which are often sold to France and Spain at high prices. Some species previously regarded as unsaleable and thrown back overboard, such as the monkfish, now form a large part of export consignments. Megrim soles sell well in Spain where they feature on most restaurant menus, but there is almost no interest in them in the UK.

To increase landings of monkfish and of the megrim, Dover and lemon soles which fetch the highest prices on the Newlyn and Looe fish markets, a new type of beam trawl is extensively used, which directs all bottom-living specimens into a large net following behind the beam. Mono-filament nets (made from tough transparent nylon line) are used for wreck fishing, especially for hake, cod, coley, pollack and ling.

In an effort to conserve stocks in the face of such efficient technology, there are periodic restrictions and quotas on certain species. Fishing in certain sea areas is also barred from time to time, particularly for pelagic species but often for cod and coley. The effect of these measures is not always what is intended: when a quota is in force, fishermen are expected to discard from nets of mixed fish all the quota fish, regardless of size. Bottom dwelling fish are already dead by the time they come aboard, so it is hard to see how throwing them back helps conserve the species.

There have been admirable improvements lately both in keeping fish on board and handling and packing fish once it has been sold on the local market. Many boats have refrigerated fish rooms where flake ice, superior in quality to the traditional lump ice, is used. Newlyn is fortunate in having

The Newlyn beam trawler *Aaltje Adriaantje* sailing out of Mount's Bay. Built in Holland in 1970, this vessel is probably the West Country's most successful beam trawler

In East Cornwall, industrial fishing in the 1990s is confined to East Looe (above) where tourists can still wander along the fish quays and see the catch landed; the boats here are mainly small trawlers and 'netters'. At villages such as Polperro (below) the fish caught is mainly for local consumption

Newlyn Fish Market in the early 1980s

the firm of W Stevenson & Sons providing pure, clean, tested water from a private underground source which feeds their works and produces ice of the highest quality.

Another innovation is the use of polystyrene boxes which keep the temperature down within the box, reflecting away external heat. They are however less sturdy than a cardboard or wooden box, and there is no environmentally friendly way of disposing of the box after use, although re-use is forbidden. Plastic boxes can be used, but there are problems in returning them to their owners; plastic can be cleaned to the satisfaction of the Health Officer.

Although the railway still terminates at Penzance, it is now rarely used as a method of transport for fish. There are no special fish wagons any longer, and without special wagons, containers and staff, modern health regulations make this method of transport difficult. Road transport has therefore replaced the railway. Refrigerated lorries, new motorways and modern shops and markets have all contributed to the efficient sales, marketing and distribution network, and further improvements to vehicles, premises and the presentation of fish are raising the perception of the fish trade to even higher levels.

Hygiene, presentation and reliability are high in the priorities of today's consumers. This means in some cases attractive packaging, sell-by dates,

Health regulations in the 1990s demand high standards of hygiene in food-handling premises, as here at Channel Foods, Newham, Truro, in the smoking of mackerel fillets

exciting books and leaflets on fish cookery, and a movement away from the 'smelly fish shop' image of the past. This is already being achieved, accompanied by a natural rise in the price of various species of fish. Consumers cannot really expect fish to be noticeably cheaper than other types of food. The annual consumption of fish per head in Britain is less than that in any other Western country, which is one reason why the export of fish from Britain is continually increasing.

The present Cornish fishing industry is predominantly that of Newlyn, where there are some fifty trawlers based, perhaps half a dozen regular Irish visitors, and a few others who come occasionally to land catches. Whereas in the late 1970s there were between 100 and 150 small boats fishing for mackerel, there are now less than ten. Of the working trawlers, about half are privately owned, and the rest are owned by W Stevenson & Sons, who are also the leading auctioneers. The crews are almost all self-employed share fishermen: there are some 500-600 men (and no women) in full time fishing, many of them the sons of fishermen, but it is doubtful if many of their sons will follow them. Now they have a choice, where for their ancestors there was none.

The future shape of the Cornish fishing industry, and even its existence in years to come, will depend on what consumers in Britain and the rest of Europe want of it, and that at present would seem to be fish of the highest quality.